Aluminium

and the Group 3 Elements

THE PERIODIC TABLE

Nigel Saunders

www.heinemann.co.uk/library
Visit our website to find out more information about Heinemann Library books.

To order:
☎ Phone 44 (0) 1865 888066
▤ Send a fax to 44 (0) 1865 314091
▢ Visit the Heinemann Bookshop at www.heinemann.co.uk/library to browse our catalogue and order online.

First published in Great Britain by Heinemann Library, Halley Court, Jordan Hill, Oxford OX2 8EJ, part of Harcourt Education. Heinemann is a registered trademark of Harcourt Education Ltd.

Produced for Heinemann by Discovery Books Ltd.

Editorial: Dr Carol Usher and Sarah Eason
Design: Ian Winton
Illustrations: Peter Bull and Stefan Chabluk
Picture Research: Vashti Gwynn
Production: Edward Moore

Originated by Ambassador Litho Ltd
Printed and bound in Hong Kong, China by South China Printing Company

ISBN 0 431 16995 0
08 07 06 05 04
10 9 8 7 6 5 4 3 2 1

British Library Cataloguing in Publication Data
Saunders, N. (Nigel)
   Aluminium and the group 3 elements.
   - (The periodic table)
   546.6'7
A full catalogue record for this book is available from the British Library.

Acknowledgements
The publishers would like to thank the following for permission to reproduce photographs:
Steve Behr p4, Corbis pp9 (George Hall), 14 top, 46 (Lester V Bergman), 16 (Duomo), 22 (Francis G. Mayer), 23 (Alain Nogues), 28 (Jeremy Horner), 30 (Yann Arthus-Bertrand), 31 (Carin Krasner), 34 (Arthur Beck), 35 (James L Amos), 36 (Nigel Rolstone, Cordaiy Photo Library Ltd.), 37 (Hulton-Deutsch Collection), 40 (Will & Deni McIntyre), 41 (Michael Heron), 45 (George D Lepp), 49 (David Lees), 50 (Patrick Allen), 51 (Rob Lewine), 52 (Bettmann), 55 (NASA); Science Photo Library pp8 (Ben Johnson), 10 (Volker Steger), 11 (Tek Image), 12, 13, 38, 44 (David Parker), 14 bottom (Sheila Terry), 17 (Tony Craddock), 19 (Vaughan Melzer), 21 (Novosti), 25 (Colin Cuthbert), 27 (Adrienne Hart-Davis) 29, 33 (Charles D Winters), 39 (Princess Margaret Rose Orthopaedic Hospital), 42 (Russ Lappa), 43 (Ben Johnson), 47 (TH Foto-Werbung), 48 (Custom Medical Stock Photo), 56, 57 (CNRI)

Cover photograph of crushed aluminium cans for recycling, reproduced with permission of Corbis.

The author would like to thank Angela, Kathryn, David and Jean for all their help and support.

Every effort has been made to contact copyright holders of any material reproduced in this book. Any omissions will be rectified in subsequent printings if notice is given to the publishers.

Disclaimer
All the Internet addresses (URLs) given in this book were valid at the time of going to press. However, due to the dynamic nature of the Internet, some addresses may have changed, or sites may have ceased to exist since publication. While the author and publishers regret any inconvenience this may cause readers, no responsibility for any such changes can be accepted by either author or the publishers.

Contents

Words appearing in bold, **like this**, are explained in the Glossary

Elements and atomic structure

All around us there are millions of different substances. If you look at your surroundings you will see plastics, metals, water and lots of other solids and liquids. We know there are gases in the air, even if we can't see them, and there are many other gases besides. The list of substances is enormous, but incredibly they all have one thing in common. They are all made from just a few simple components, called **elements**.

Elements and compounds

Elements are substances that cannot be broken down into anything simpler using chemical **reactions**. There are ninety-two naturally occurring elements and scientists have discovered how to make over twenty more using **nuclear reactions**. About three-quarters of the elements are metals, such as aluminium, and the rest are non-metals, such as oxygen. The elements can join together in countless combinations in chemical reactions to make **compounds**. Aluminium and oxygen, for example, react together to make aluminium oxide, commonly called alumina. Most of the millions of different substances in the world are compounds, made up of two or more elements chemically joined together.

▼ The metal **alloy** frames, rubber tyres, riders' clothing and even the human bodies you can see in this bike race, are made from some of the millions of substances in the world. This means they are all made of chemical elements.

Atoms

Every substance, whether it is an element or a compound, is made up of tiny particles called **atoms**. An element contains just one sort of atom and compounds are made from two or more types of atom joined together. Individual atoms are far too tiny for us to see, even with a light microscope. If you could stack eight million aluminium atoms on top of each other, the pile would only be a millimetre high!

Subatomic particles

Atoms are not the smallest things in the Universe. They are made from even smaller objects called **subatomic particles**. The biggest ones, called **protons** and **neutrons**, are joined together in the centre of the atom, making a **nucleus**. Smaller subatomic particles, called '**electrons**', are arranged in layers, or 'shells' around the nucleus. This arrangement of electrons resembles the way the planets are arranged around the Sun. In fact most of an atom is empty space.

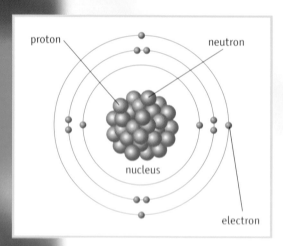

This is a model of an aluminium atom. Each one contains 13 protons and 14 neutrons, with 13 electrons arranged in three shells, or energy levels, around the nucleus.

Groups

Chemistry is both exciting and puzzling because elements all react differently. To help make sense of the reactions, several attempts were made to organize the elements. A Russian chemist called Dimitri Mendeleev was the most successful. In 1869, he placed each element into one of eight **groups** within a table, making sure that he put similar elements into each group. This made it much easier for chemists to work out how elements might react with each other. The modern **periodic table** is based closely on Mendeleev's table.

CHAPTER 2

The periodic table, aluminium and the group 3 elements

Chemists have built upon Mendeleev's table and it has gradually evolved into the **periodic table** we know today. The **elements** are arranged in horizontal rows called **periods**, with the **atomic number** (number of **protons** in the **nucleus**) increasing from left to right. Each vertical column in the periodic table is called a **group**. The atomic number of the elements increases as you go down a group and the elements in each group have similar chemical properties. There are eighteen groups altogether.

The number of **electrons** an element has and the way they are arranged in their shells determines how it **reacts**. All the elements in a group have the same number of electrons in the shell furthest from the nucleus, which is called the outer shell. The elements in group 1, for instance, are very reactive metals with one electron in their outer shells, whereas the elements in group 7 are reactive non-metals with seven electrons in their outer shells. The periodic table gets its

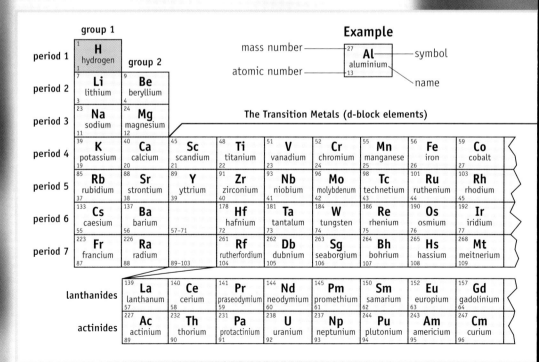

name because these different chemical properties recur regularly or periodically.

The properties of the elements change gradually as you go down a group. In group 2 the elements become more reactive. When beryllium, which is at the top of the group, is added to water it does not react at all; calcium, in the middle of the group, slowly produces bubbles of hydrogen; while barium, near the bottom of the group, produces lots of bubbles.

Aluminium and the group 3 elements

The first element in group 3, boron, is a metalloid, which means that it has some of the properties of metals and some of the properties of non-metals. The rest of the elements in the group; aluminium, gallium, indium and thallium, are metals. In this book, you are going to find out about them and many of their uses.

▼ *This is the periodic table of the elements. Group 3 contains boron, aluminium, gallium, indium and thallium. These elements are all metals apart from boron, which is a metalloid.*

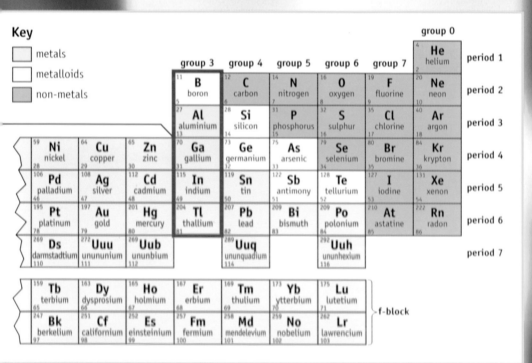

Key

☐ metals
☐ metalloids
☐ non-metals

	group 3	group 4	group 5	group 6	group 7	group 0	
						4 **He** helium 2	period 1
	11 **B** boron 5	12 **C** carbon 6	14 **N** nitrogen 7	16 **O** oxygen 8	19 **F** fluorine 9	20 **Ne** neon 10	period 2
	27 **Al** aluminium 13	28 **Si** silicon 14	31 **P** phosphorus 15	32 **S** sulphur 16	35 **Cl** chlorine 17	40 **Ar** argon 18	period 3
59 **Ni** nickel 28 / 64 **Cu** copper 29 / 65 **Zn** zinc 30	70 **Ga** gallium 31	73 **Ge** germanium 32	75 **As** arsenic 33	79 **Se** selenium 34	80 **Br** bromine 35	84 **Kr** krypton 36	period 4
106 **Pd** palladium 46 / 108 **Ag** silver 47 / 112 **Cd** cadmium 48	115 **In** indium 49	119 **Sn** tin 50	122 **Sb** antimony 51	128 **Te** tellurium 52	127 **I** iodine 53	131 **Xe** xenon 54	period 5
195 **Pt** platinum 78 / 197 **Au** gold 79 / 201 **Hg** mercury 80	204 **Tl** thallium 81	207 **Pb** lead 82	209 **Bi** bismuth 83	209 **Po** polonium 84	210 **At** astatine 85	222 **Rn** radon 86	period 6
269 **Ds** darmstadtium 110 / 272 **Uuu** unununium 111 / 269 **Uub** ununbium 112		289 **Uuq** ununquadium 114		292 **Uuh** ununhexium 116			period 7

159 **Tb** terbium 65	163 **Dy** dysprosium 66	165 **Ho** holmium 67	167 **Er** erbium 68	169 **Tm** thulium 69	173 **Yb** ytterbium 70	175 **Lu** lutetium 71	f-block
247 **Bk** berkelium 97	251 **Cf** californium 98	252 **Es** einsteinium 99	257 **Fm** fermium 100	258 **Md** mendelevium 101	259 **No** nobelium 102	262 **Lr** lawrencium 103	

Elements of group 3

The **group** 3 **elements** are boron, aluminium, gallium, indium and thallium. They are all metals except boron. Going down the group, from boron to thallium, their boiling points decrease and their **densities** increase dramatically. The group 3 elements are all solids at room temperature, but gallium has a very low melting point compared to the rest. If you hold some gallium in your hand it melts and becomes a liquid.

11	**B**	boron
5	boron	symbol: B • atomic number: 5 • metalloid

What does it look like? Boron exists in several forms, including hard, grey crystals and a brown powder. Boron does not **react** with oxygen in the air, unless it is heated strongly, nor does it react with water or hydrochloric acid. However, it will react with concentrated sulphuric acid and nitric acid. Boron is a good conductor at high temperatures, but not at room temperature.

Where is it found? Boron exists naturally as a **compound**, but not as a pure element because it is too reactive. It is found all over the world in various **minerals** such as borax, kernite and colemanite. It was named by joining the first part of the word borax with the last part of the word carbon.

This is a piece of kernite. It contains boron in a compound called sodium tetraborate. Kernite is soft and very light. ▶

What are its main uses? Boron itself has very few uses, but its compounds have many. Boron nitride is a hard substance used in abrasives and other compounds are found in fibreglass, heat-resistant glass, detergents and fireworks.

27 Al aluminium 13	**aluminium**
	symbol: Al • atomic number: 13 • metal

What does it look like?   Aluminium is a strong, silvery metal. It is very malleable, which means that it is easy to shape. It has a low density, so pieces of aluminium feel light for their size. Although aluminium is a very reactive metal, when covered by a layer of aluminium oxide it stops reacting with air or water. However, it will react with hydrochloric acid and sulphuric acid, especially if it is heated.

Where is it found?   Aluminium is the most abundant metal in the Earth's crust, but is too reactive to be found as a pure metal. It is present in many minerals including bauxite and cryolite. Bauxite, which contains aluminium oxide, is its main **ore**.

What are its main uses?   Aluminium and its **alloys** have many uses such as building aircraft, bicycles and window frames; containers to store drinks and food; and aluminium cables, which conduct electricity over long distances. Precious stones, such as rubies and sapphires, are made from aluminium compounds. Other compounds are used in water treatment plants, antiperspirants and medicines to help upset stomachs.

▼ *Strong aluminium alloys are used to make aircraft such as this Boeing 730-330. These alloys are strong and have a low density, so they help to reduce the weight of the aircraft.*

N949WP

More elements of group 3

70	
Ga	
gallium	
31	

gallium
symbol: Ga • atomic number: 31 • metal

What does it look like?   Gallium is a soft, silvery metal that is solid at room temperature, but becomes a liquid above 29.7 °C. Gallium **reacts** slowly with damp air at first, forming a layer of gallium oxide on its surface that stops it reacting any further. This layer also prevents gallium reacting with water, but it still reacts slowly with hydrochloric acid.

Where is it found?   Gallium occurs widely in the Earth's crust in its **compounds**. These are found in small amounts in many **minerals**, including bauxite (aluminium **ore**).

What are its main uses?   Many gallium compounds, especially gallium arsenide, are important **semiconductor** materials. These materials are used in a huge range of everyday electronic products, including CD players and solar cells that power calculators.

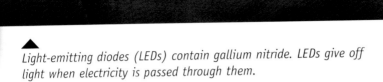

▲
Light-emitting diodes (LEDs) contain gallium nitride. LEDs give off light when electricity is passed through them.

115	
In	
indium	
49	

indium
symbol: In • atomic number: 49 • metal

What does it look like?   Indium is another silvery metal that is very soft. It does not react with air unless it is heated strongly or with water, but it does react with acids.

Where is it found?   Indium does not exist as a free metal in the Earth's crust. There are no indium minerals, but small amounts of indium compounds are present in many minerals, especially zinc ores.

What are its main uses?   Indium **alloys** are used in lead-free solders that join electronic components together. Indium compounds are used in the liquid crystal displays found in many everyday items such as digital watches and electronic games.

◄ The liquid crystal displays (LCDs) used in electronic devices, like cellphones, CD players and digital watches have a layer of transparent indium-tin oxide, which conducts electricity.

204	Tl	**thallium**
81	thallium	symbol: Tl • atomic number: 81 • metal

What does it look like?   Thallium is a bluish, silvery metal that is soft enough to cut with a knife. It reacts slowly with oxygen in the air to form a thick layer of blue-grey thallium oxide. Thallium reacts slowly with water and acids.

Where is it found?   Thallium is found in a few rare minerals such as lorandite (thallium arsenic sulphide) and is usually **extracted** as a by-product of zinc production.

What are its main uses?   Thallium metal has no commercial uses, but its compounds are used in **radiation** detectors and special glass that has a very low melting point.

Discovering elements with light

Two German chemists, Gustav Kirchhoff and Robert Bunsen, discovered caesium in 1860 by analyzing the light it emits. Three metals in group 3, gallium, indium and thallium, were discovered within fourteen years of each other using this method, which is known as **spectroscopy**.

This is Gustav Kirchhoff (1824–1887). Working with Robert Bunsen, he discovered caesium and rubidium by studying the spectra of light given off by compounds when they are heated strongly. ▶

Flame tests

Kirchhoff was the first person to realize that metals produce different colours when their **compounds** are burnt in a flame. Flame tests allow chemists to work out which metal is in an unknown compound. In a flame test, some of the compound is put on a loop of clean platinum wire and held in the hottest part of the Bunsen burner flame. The colour of the resulting flame depends upon the metal in the compound.

Excited electrons

When an **atom** is heated, its **electrons** use the extra energy to jump into a shell further from the **nucleus**. Electrons cannot stay in this 'excited' state for long and soon fall back to a shell closer to the nucleus. They give off their extra energy as light; big falls give out blue light and small falls give out red light. Each **element** produces different colours because its electrons can make different jumps and falls.

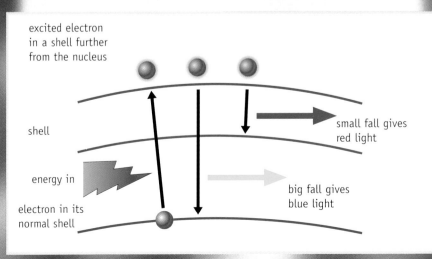

excited electron in a shell further from the nucleus

shell

energy in

electron in its normal shell

small fall gives red light

big fall gives blue light

Spectroscopy

In spectroscopy, the light given off in a flame test is analyzed using a device called a spectroscope. The simplest spectroscope contains a **prism** to split light from the flame into its **spectrum**. Each element produces a unique spectrum of colours, similar to a coloured barcode. Kirchhoff and Bunsen discovered caesium when they found some compounds that produced a spectrum they had not seen before. They named the new metal after the Latin for word for sky blue, because its spectrum contains two blue lines.

Prisms and light

Sir Isaac Newton investigated light in the seventeenth century. He discovered that white light is made from the colours of the rainbow. Newton found that a prism splits light up into a spectrum, displaying the different colours it contains.

◀ *White light is a mixture of all the different colours we see. When a beam of white light is shone through a glass prism, the light is split up to make a spectrum.*

Gallium, indium and thallium

Sir William Crookes discovered thallium in 1861. He named the new metal after the Greek word meaning a green twig because its spectrum contained a clear green line. Indium was discovered two years later by the German chemists, Ferdinand Reich and Theodor Richter. Indium is named after the Latin word for indigo because its spectrum contained an indigo or very dark blue line.

Paul-Emile Lecoq, a French chemist, discovered gallium in 1875. Although gallium's spectrum contains violet lines, Lecoq named the element after the Latin word for France, which is Gallia.

Boron

Boron is a metalloid, which means that it has some properties of metals and some of non-metals. For instance, it is a poor conductor of electricity at room temperature, but a good conductor at high temperatures and it can **react** with both metals and non-metals. Boron reacts with concentrated sulphuric acid and nitric acid, but not with hydrochloric acid or water. It only reacts with oxygen in the air if it is heated strongly. There are several forms of boron, including a dull brown powder and shiny grey crystals.

These are shiny grey pieces of crystalline boron. Compounds containing boron are found in heat-resistant glass, detergents and the control rods for nuclear power stations. ▶

Discovery of boron

Boron was discovered in 1808, but boron **compounds** such as borax have been used for hundreds of years. Boron was discovered twice. Sir Humphry Davy, an English chemist, heated potassium with boric acid and produced brown powdered boron. At nearly the same time, two French chemists, Joseph-Louis Gay-Lussac and Louis-Jacques Thénard, carried out similar experiments. Davy called the new **element** boracium and the French called it *bore*.

This is the French chemist, Joseph-Louis Gay-Lussac (1778–1850), who was one of the first chemists to isolate boron. ▶

After studying the new element's chemical reactions, Davy decided that it was not a metal after all, so its name should not end in –ium. (This word ending usually indicates a metal. The exception is 'helium', a non-metal.) Four years later Davy suggested the name boron because it is similar to carbon.

Davy's experiments with electricity

An Italian scientist, called Alessandro Volta, invented the electric battery at the end of the eighteenth century. Humphry Davy was one of the first chemists to find out what happens when electricity is passed through different substances. After building his own battery, Davy used it to discover sodium and potassium in 1807 and to isolate magnesium, calcium, strontium and barium a year later. Davy also isolated some boron in 1808 by passing electricity through boric acid.

Extracting boron

On average, every tonne of rock contains 9 g of boron. It is found in various **minerals**, such as borax, colemanite and kernite. Some natural spring water contains boric acid. Boron minerals have many uses and to **extract** the relatively little boron they contain requires several steps. These include heating boron oxide with magnesium to produce impure powdery boron.

The word equation for producing boron from boron oxide is:

boron oxide + magnesium ⟶ boron + magnesium oxide

If very pure crystals of boron are needed, boron chloride is heated with hydrogen using very hot wires.

The word equation for producing boron from boron chloride is:

boron chloride + hydrogen ⟶ boron + hydrogen chloride

Uses of boron

Powdered boron burns with a green flame and is used in fireworks and green signal flares. However, boron has lots of other uses, including the production of advanced composite materials and **alloys**.

Boron fibres

Very fine boron fibres can be used to produce extremely tough, lightweight materials. They are made by heating very fine tungsten wires in a mixture of boron chloride and hydrogen at over 1000 °C. Boron chloride and hydrogen **react** to produce tiny crystals of pure boron, which form on the tungsten wires. The boron fibres are usually about 0.1 mm in diameter – about as thick as a human hair. They cannot be used on their own, but must be set in another substance, like metal or plastic.

Composite materials

Composite materials are made by combining two very different materials to produce a new substance. Usually this substance has better properties than either material on its own. Resin, for example, may be too weak to make a tennis racquet, but when combined with boron fibres it forms a strong, lightweight material.

Boron fibres set in various plastic resins are used in aircraft, the hulls of racing boats and sports equipment, such as fishing rods, golf clubs and tennis racquets. The frame of the Space Shuttle is made from aluminium tubes reinforced with boron fibres. This material is stronger and stiffer than aluminium, so less of it is needed and the weight of the tubes is nearly halved. This allows the shuttle to carry a bigger payload into space.

Boron in alloys

Most of the metals we see around us are not pure metals, but alloys. These are mixtures of different metals or metals mixed with non-metals or **compounds**. The alloys produced by adding boron or boron compounds to metals are usually harder than the metals alone. Steel mixed with boron and titanium produces a very tough alloy that is often used for security chains, such as the expensive chains that go with bicycle locks. Large earth-moving vehicles and excavators need tough metal blades to scrape away soil. The steel used in these blades contains tiny amounts of boron to increase its strength and toughness.

◀ Boron steel is tougher and stronger than ordinary steel, so it is used in the blades of excavators and other earth-moving equipment.

Aluminium is widely used to make high-voltage electricity cables. However, its ability to conduct electricity is reduced if it contains even small amounts of other metals, such as iron and titanium. If boron is added in the right amounts to react with these impurities, a slag is produced that is easily separated from the aluminium.

◀ Tennis racquets (opposite) and other sports equipment such as golf clubs and fishing rods may be strengthened with boron fibres set in special plastic resins.

Boron and nuclear reactions

Boron is very good at absorbing **neutrons** produced by **nuclear reactions**, which makes it especially useful for controlling the **reactions** in nuclear reactors.

Neutrons will break us apart

Chemical reactions involve the **electrons** around the **nucleus**, but nuclear reactions involve the nucleus itself. Nuclear fission is the type of nuclear reaction used in nuclear reactors. This is when **atoms** in the reactor's nuclear fuel split apart. Uranium is used as a nuclear fuel because its atoms can be split apart relatively easily.

When a uranium atom splits it produces two smaller atoms, some heat and **radiation**, and two or three neutrons. These neutrons shoot out at high speed and smash into other uranium atoms. These atoms may split too, producing even more neutrons. This is called a chain reaction and must be controlled, otherwise so much energy is released in a short time that a nuclear explosion happens.

Controlling the reaction

A nuclear reaction will carry on at a steady pace if each uranium atom that splits causes one more to split. When this occurs, the reaction is 'critical'. In a nuclear reactor, the reaction is controlled so that it is just critical. This is done using control rods made from boron steel or boron carbide. Boron absorbs neutrons, stopping them splitting uranium atoms. If the boron control rods are lowered right into the reactor, the boron absorbs so many neutrons that the chain reaction stops. However, they are usually lifted out of the reactor until the reaction just keeps going.

The first nuclear reactor

The first nuclear reactor was built at the University of Chicago and started up on 2 December 1942. An Italian-American physicist called Enrico Fermi led the team that built it. Element number 100 is called fermium in his honour.

Boron effectively slows down the neutrons produced in nuclear reactions by absorbing them. These are some of the 211 boron carbide control rods used in the nuclear power station near Chernobyl in the Ukraine. When too few of these were left in the reactor in April 1986, disaster ensued.

Nuclear reactors and electricity

The heat produced by the nuclear reaction is used to boil water to make steam. This drives turbines, just like a conventional power station running on coal, gas or oil. The turbines turn electricity generators and provide factories and millions of homes with electricity. Over several months, the nuclear fuel is slowly used up and the reaction slows down. The boron control rods are gradually lifted higher to keep the reaction going, until some of the spent fuel must be replaced. If anything goes wrong with the reactor the boron control rods drop down automatically, stopping the reaction within seconds.

Life-saving boron

The **nuclear reaction** in a reactor is controlled by lowering or raising control rods that contain boron. If the control rods are lifted out, the reaction goes faster and if they are lowered, it slows down. However, what would happen if nearly all the control rods were lifted out at once?

The Chernobyl disaster

The Chernobyl nuclear power station was 15 km (9.5 miles) from Chernobyl, a town 100 km (62 miles) north of Kiev in the Ukraine. Mistakes made by the operators during an experiment combined with a design fault in the reactor caused the nuclear reaction to destabilize.

The reactor used 211 boron carbide control rods and at least 30 had to be in the reactor for it to be safe. At one point, early in the morning of 26 April 1986, the operators left only eight boron carbide control rods in the reactor and the nuclear reaction went out of control. All the control rods were dropped back into the reactor, but this pushed cooling water out of the way, making things worse. An enormous amount of heat was produced, which melted the uranium fuel and turned the water to steam. The pressure from the steam caused an explosion that wrecked the reactor and blew off its lid. This weighed one thousand tonnes. Graphite in the core of the reactor ignited and released huge amounts of **radioactive** chemicals that were carried by winds and air currents throughout Europe and beyond.

Boron to the rescue

It took several days to put the fires out at the Chernobyl reactor. Helicopters dumped a mixture of boron carbide, lead, sand and other materials over the fire. The boron carbide captured **neutrons** to stop any nuclear reactions and the lead absorbed the **radiation.** Nearly 1000 people were involved in fire-fighting and 800,000 soldiers helped clean up after the accident. Many of these people and the local population received large radiation doses. Radiation damages cells and the **DNA** in them, causing illnesses such as cancer. There were some deaths and many people still suffer from illnesses linked to the radiation.

▲
These are the remains of the Chernobyl nuclear power station after it exploded in the early hours of 26 April 1986.

Killing cancer cells

Boron neutron capture therapy (BNCT) is a treatment for cancer. Doctors inject the patient with a boron **compound** that concentrates in cancer cells. A machine called a particle accelerator is used to fire neutrons at the cancer. When a boron **atom** in a cancer cell absorbs a neutron, it splits in two and gives off alpha radiation. This type of radiation does not travel far, so the cancer cells are killed, but not the healthy cells around them.

Borates

Boron forms several different **compounds** with oxygen, including borax and boric acid. These different compounds can be converted into each other and in industry the word 'borates' is used loosely for all of them.

Borax

Borax is the common name for sodium tetraborate decahydrate ($Na_2B_4O_7.10H_2O$). A colourless solid with a soft, slippery feel, it is the most important source of boron compounds. Nearly half the world's borax comes from California, USA. Boric acid (H_3BO_3) is made by **reacting** concentrated borax solution with hydrochloric acid. Boric oxide (B_2O_3) is formed when boric acid is heated. These compounds and others, such as sodium perborate ($NaBO_3$), have a great many uses.

Tincal

*In the Middle Ages, borax was **extracted** from salt lakes in Tibet. It was called tincal and used to make pottery glazes.*

Glazes

Pottery and tiles are covered with a hard, glassy substance called a glaze. These are usually coloured, smooth and shiny, giving the object an attractive, tough finish that is difficult to scratch. Borates are added to help the pigments dissolve in the glaze, to stick glaze to the pottery and to make it more resistant to water and cleaning chemicals.

The glazes used on tiles and pottery, like this vase, contain boron compounds. They produce a smooth, tough finish that resists water and cleaning fluids.

Steel and other metals can be coated with a tough type of glaze called enamel that also contains borates. Enamelled steel sheet is used to make the sides of washing machines and dishwashers. Other utensils found in the kitchen may be enamelled, such as pans, coffeepots and kettles; hikers and campers often use enamelled cups and plates.

Helping keep clean

Borates are widely used in household detergents and soaps, including those for washing machines and dishwashers. They soften the water, which improves the cleaning power of the detergent and prevents sticky 'scum' forming. Sodium perborate may be added as a bleach, to remove stains from clothes and dishes. Shampoos, bath salts and liquid soaps contain borates that improve the consistency as well as removing oils and other dirt.

Glass and glass fibres

Borosilicate glass is very tough and heat-resistant. It is made by adding boric acid to sand, which is the main ingredient for making glass. This type of glass is used to make beakers and test tubes for chemistry laboratories and kitchen glassware, such as jugs, bowls and ovenware. The biggest single use for borates is in the manufacture of glass fibres. These are very fine strands of glass, made by squeezing molten glass through small holes. Glass fibre is used as heat insulation in homes and woven glass fibres are mixed with plastic resins to make fibreglass objects, such as canoes and surfboards.

◀ *Boron compounds are widely used in the manufacture of glass fibres. These are used to insulate buildings and to make tough fibreglass objects such as baths and boats.*

Borates and black diamonds

Boron can form complex **compounds** with hydrogen, called boranes. Diborane (B_2H_6) is a poisonous and explosive gas, which is used by computer chip manufacturers to provide the tiny amounts of boron required by some silicon chips.

Boron carbide is used in the control rods for nuclear power stations because it is good at absorbing **neutrons**, but it has other important properties.

Black diamond

Boron carbide is made by heating boron oxide with carbon in a furnace. It is sometimes called 'black diamond' because it is very hard, like real diamond, and is a good abrasive. Manufacturers of computer hard disk drives use boron carbide for polishing disks. Nozzles for sandblasting hoses, bullet-proof seats for helicopters and armoured tiles for military vehicles are also made from it. Boron carbide body armour is much lighter than similar armour made from other materials, such as steel. Boron carbide is also mixed with metals to produce very hard **alloys** that are used to make tough cutting blades.

The word equation for the manufacture of boron carbide is:

boron oxide + carbon → boron carbide + carbon monoxide

Boric acid (H_3BO_3) may be used instead of boron oxide.

White graphite

Boron chloride heated with ammonia (NH_3) makes boron nitride. Like boron carbide, boron nitride resists attack from other chemicals and has a high melting point. It has a slippery feel and makes a good lubricant, so it is sometimes called 'white graphite'. Real graphite is a form of pure carbon used in pencils because layers of graphite slide on to paper leaving a mark. Powdered boron nitride is used in cosmetics to produce a silky feel in face powders and lipsticks. Boron nitride is a good conductor of heat and it is an important component of thermal pastes used for computer chips.

Modern computer chips generate a lot of heat as they work. If this heat is not removed from the chip, the computer may not function properly and some very fast chips may even catch fire! To prevent this, a 'heat sink' is attached to the surface of the chip. A typical heat sink has spikes or vanes to conduct heat away and is often made from aluminium because this is lightweight and a good heat conductor. Thermal paste, containing boron nitride powder, is smeared over the surface of the chip before the heat sink is attached to it, ensuring that heat is conducted from the chip to the heat sink efficiently.

The processor chips in modern computers produce large amounts of waste heat. This is carried away from the chips using aluminium heat sinks and fans. Special paste that contains boron nitride helps to conduct heat from the chips to the heat sinks efficiently.

Boron in living things

Plants and animals need boron to stay healthy, but only in small amounts, as some boron **compounds** are poisonous, especially those that dissolve in water.

Fertilizers and herbicides

Plants need boron to help them transport sugars and make cell walls. When there is not enough boron in the soil the fruits, stems, leaves or roots of a plant may crack on the surface and rot in the centre. The heads of cauliflowers turn dark, for example. Farmers use artificial **fertilizers** containing boron compounds on soil that does not contain enough boron. Plants can only absorb **minerals** through their roots if they are dissolved in water and so fertilizers usually contain soluble boron compounds such as sodium borate and borax. However, farmers need to add just the right amount of these fertilizers because too much boron will poison the plants, turning the leaves yellow. Some valuable crops, such as grapes and strawberries, are particularly sensitive to excess boron. In fact boric acid and other boron compounds are used in **herbicides**, which are chemicals that kill weeds.

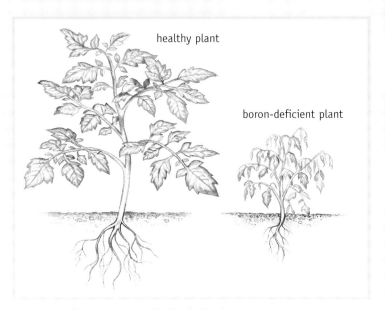

healthy plant

boron-deficient plant

▲
If there is not enough boron in the soil, the walls around plant cells do not form properly and the plants do not grow very well.

Boron in our diet

Too much boron is poisonous, but tiny amounts of it are needed in our diet. Many foods are rich in boron, including  raisins, peanuts, popcorn and chocolate, so we are unlikely to suffer from boron deficiency. Unlike many other trace minerals, no particular symptoms of boron deficiency are known and there is no recommended daily dose. However, there is some evidence that boron may protect us from arthritis. This is a disease that makes our joints inflamed, painful and difficult to move. On average fewer people seem to suffer from arthritis in areas where the diet is naturally rich in boron, whereas in areas with little boron in the soil, more people seem to suffer from it. However, there is no medical evidence overall that suggests we should deliberately take extra boron in our diet to stay healthy.

◀ *Some foods, such as chocolate, raisins and peanuts are rich sources of boron.*

Sick of boron

Excessive exposure to boron can cause diarrhoea and peeling red skin. Large amounts of it cause low blood pressure, vomiting and hair loss. Although this is unlikely to happen in our everyday lives, people who handle boron compounds in their jobs wear masks and gloves and there are regulations to ensure that boron compounds are disposed of properly.

Pests and pesticides

Boric acid is used in some **pesticides**. These are chemicals that kill undesirable insects such as cockroaches, ants and termites. When the insects walk through the pesticide powder, it sticks to their legs and is swallowed when they clean themselves.

Aluminium

Aluminium is a strong, silvery metal that is malleable and has a low **density**. Its surface is covered with a very thin, transparent layer of aluminium oxide that stops the aluminium **reacting** with air or water. However, aluminium will react with hydrochloric acid, especially if it is heated. Powdered aluminium will burn with orange sparks if it is sprinkled into a Bunsen burner flame.

This is the famous Statue of Eros at Piccadilly Circus in London. It was cast from aluminium in 1893, when aluminium was still regarded as a rare, expensive and new metal. ▶

Saved by the oxide

A very thin, transparent layer of aluminium oxide naturally forms on the surface of aluminium and sticks tightly to the metal. This stops oxygen and water reaching the metal beneath, so aluminium seems to be less reactive than it really is. When pieces of aluminium are dropped into warm hydrochloric acid, nothing seems to happen at first. However, the acid reacts with the protective layer and removes it. Once the metal is exposed, it reacts vigorously with the acid, producing aluminium chloride and lots of hydrogen gas bubbles.

Discovery of aluminium

Aluminium **compounds** have been used for thousands of years. Potassium aluminium sulphate forms a crystalline substance called alum, which was widely used to help dyes stick to cloth. Chemists were confident that alum and other compounds really did contain a new metal. Aluminium was finally discovered in 1825 by the Danish chemist, Hans Christian Oersted, when he heated some aluminium chloride with potassium dissolved in mercury.

The word equation for the extraction of aluminium using potassium is:

$$\text{aluminium chloride} + \text{potassium} \rightarrow \text{aluminium} + \text{potassium chloride}$$

The reaction happens because potassium is more reactive than aluminium and displaces aluminium from its compounds.

You say aluminum ...

The new metal was first named alumium after the Latin word for the crystals we call alum. Its name later changed to aluminum (as used in the USA now) and then became aluminium. In 1925, the American Chemical Society decided to stick with aluminum. The rest of the English-speaking world calls it aluminium and since 1990, this has been the spelling recommended by IUPAC (the International Union of Pure and Applied Chemistry).

Abundant aluminium

Aluminium is the most abundant metal and forms 8.2 per cent of the Earth's crust. It is found in various **minerals** such as bauxite and cryolite. Aluminium is difficult to **extract** from its compounds because it is a reactive metal.

◀ The Danish scientist, Hans Christian Oersted (1777–1851), is seen here with an assistant, working on an experiment involving electricity and magnetism. Oersted discovered aluminium in 1825.

Aluminium extraction and recycling

Bauxite is aluminium's main **ore** and contains aluminium oxide. It is mined in huge quantities, mainly in South America, the Caribbean, Australia and Africa. Over twenty-four million tonnes of aluminium are produced each year worldwide.

Alumina

Bauxite contains other substances as well as aluminium oxide, which have to be removed. In the Bayer process, the bauxite is treated with sodium hydroxide solution to produce a white powder called alumina. This is purified aluminium oxide. The waste material mostly contains iron oxide and sand. It is called 'red mud' because of its colour.

▲
This huge bauxite mine is in Venezuela in South America. Much of the land disturbed by the world's bauxite mines was originally covered by forests, but with care new trees can be planted after a mine closes.

Pass the electricity

Aluminium is **extracted** using **electrolysis**. This involves passing electricity through molten alumina, causing it to break down into aluminium and oxygen. Unfortunately, alumina has a very high melting point (over 2000 °C). A lot of energy would be needed to reach this temperature, so the alumina is dissolved in a **mineral** called cryolite, which melts at a much lower temperature.

Cryolite

Cryolite (Na_3AlF_6) is a mineral that melts at just over 1000 °C. Alumina dissolves in molten cryolite and as a result does not have to be melted. This clever bit of chemistry reduces the temperature needed to extract aluminium to around 950 °C, saving energy and money.

The molten mixture of alumina and cryolite is contained in a large 'pot' lined with graphite. Graphite is a type of carbon that conducts electricity well and this forms the negative electrode. Graphite blocks lowered into the pot form the positive electrodes. An electric current is passed through the molten mixture between the lining and the blocks. This causes molten aluminium to form at the lining while oxygen gas bubbles off at the positive electrode. The metal sinks to the bottom of the pot from where it is removed, cooled and solidified.

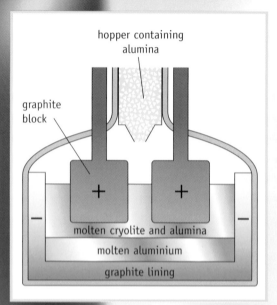

hopper containing alumina

graphite block

+ +

− −

molten cryolite and alumina

molten aluminium

graphite lining

◀ *This diagram shows how aluminium is extracted by electrolysis.*

Expensive aluminium

Even though there is a lot of aluminium in the Earth's crust, it is expensive. This is because sixteen kilowatt-hours of electricity – enough to run a hundred-watt light bulb for nearly a week – are needed to produce a kilogram of aluminium. This is why aluminium smelters are often built in areas where electricity is cheap and plentiful.

Although aluminium is extracted at 950 °C, its melting point is only 660 °C. This means that far less energy is needed to melt and recycle aluminium. Over a third of the aluminium needed is from recycled sources.

◀ *Aluminium is used to make drinks cans like these, which are collected for recycling. A lot of energy is needed to produce aluminium from its ore, so over a third of the aluminium we use comes from recycled metal.*

Uses of aluminium

Aluminium is expensive now, but in the middle of the nineteenth century it was dearer than gold. Visitors to the 1855 Paris Exhibition marvelled at an exhibit of aluminium and Napoleon III had a special set of cutlery made from the new metal, reserved only for very important visitors. Fortunately, its value fell dramatically after the Hall-Héroult process to **extract** aluminium was developed in 1886.

The Hall-Héroult process

The modern process for extracting aluminium from alumina was invented by two men working on opposite sides of the North Atlantic. Charles Hall in the USA and Paul Héroult in France came up with the idea at the same time in 1886. Not only that, they were both born in 1863 and both died in 1914!

Super-pure aluminium

If aluminium is more than 99.9 per cent pure it is called super-pure aluminium. This is a very shiny material used to make the reflective coatings on light fittings, like those used for modern, low-voltage halogen lighting. Metallic inks and paints, including those used for car bodywork, contain powdered super-pure aluminium. Different effects are achieved by varying the size and shape of the aluminium grains in the paint. Metal objects such as car wheels can be coated with aluminium to give a shiny finish, similar to chromium plating.

Into space with aluminium

The Space Shuttle and the Ariane 5 rocket both use solid rocket boosters. Each Space Shuttle booster contains about eighty tonnes of aluminium powder and the smaller Ariane 5 boosters have forty tonnes. Powdered aluminium will burn if heated to over 1000 °C in a flame. The oxygen needed for the aluminium to burn is supplied by ammonium perchlorate powder (NH_4ClO_4). The ammonium perchlorate is mixed with the aluminium powder and a chemical called butadiene is added to stick it all together.

Weld those rails

When aluminium powder is mixed with iron oxide powder and heated, they **react** to produce aluminium oxide and iron. The reaction is very vigorous with lots of flames, smoke and heat. So much heat is produced that the iron melts. This is called the thermit reaction and is useful for joining railway track rails together.

Aluminium is also used in reactions like this to extract chromium and vanadium from their **ores**.

◀ There is a very dramatic reaction between powdered aluminium and iron oxide when they are heated together. So much heat is produced that the iron formed during the reaction melts.

The word equation for the thermit reaction is:

aluminium + iron oxide → aluminium oxide + iron

Aluminium is more reactive than iron, so it is able to displace iron from iron **compounds**.

Aluminium in the home

Aluminium is usually mixed with other metals to produce **alloys** that are harder and stronger than aluminium alone and can be seen in action all around us, especially in our homes.

Hold your drink

Drinks cans are made from aluminium containing a small amount of manganese, which increases its strength and makes it easier to press into shape. Aluminium is not poisonous and does not rust, but drinks cans are usually lined with a very thin layer of plastic. This ensures that the acids and salts in beverages never come in contact with the aluminium. Aluminium has a low **density** so the cans are lighter than glass bottles or steel cans. This makes them easier to carry, saves energy when they are transported and helps when they are collected for recycling.

Eat up

Aluminium foil is very thin aluminium alloy sheet, widely used for storing and cooking food. The metal is passed through rollers until it reaches the desired thickness. Foil for a food container is around 0.07 mm thick, while household cooking foil is even thinner than this.

Aluminium foil conducts heat well and prevents moisture escaping when food is cooked in the oven. It can be wrapped around sandwiches and other foods, helping to keep them fresh. Many frozen or chilled 'ready meals' are supplied in aluminium foil containers.

Aluminium foil conducts heat well and prevents moisture escaping, so it is very useful for storing food or cooking it in the oven. ▶

Pouches for dried foods such as dehydrated soup and cartons for liquids like orange juice are made from plastic or card, lined with very thin aluminium foil. Many saucepans are made from aluminium. They are light, strong and do not rust.

A good reflector

Shiny aluminium foil is very good at reflecting heat. It is used to make emergency sleeping bags and insulating wraps for newborn babies and marathon runners. Boilers are often insulated with aluminium foil.

Light and strong

Window frames, doors and handrails can be made from aluminium and it is used to make the wall cladding in large buildings. Aluminium is easier to handle than steel because of its low density. There is no need to paint it because aluminium does not rust. Aluminium alloys containing a little scandium or beryllium for added strength are used for the frames of rucksacks, bicycles and baseball bats. Aluminium ladders are lighter than traditional wooden ones, but they should not be used near overhead electricity cables because aluminium is a good conductor of electricity.

A good conductor of electricity

Copper conducts electricity better than aluminium, but aluminium is used for overhead electricity cables because it is much lighter. It is also widely used for underground cables and cables in tall buildings. Television aerials, satellite dishes and the bases of electric light bulbs are made from aluminium as well.

◀ *Baseball bats, ladders, rucksack and bicycle frames are often made from aluminium alloys because they are light and strong.*

Travelling with aluminium

Aluminium is used in the manufacture of many types of vehicle as its low **density** lessens their weight, reduces the amount of fuel they need and helps to make them more manoeuvrable.

Aluminium alloys are also used in naval vessels and fast ferries like this one. The aluminium reduces the weight of the ship and it does not rust. ▶

On the road

Steel is often used in road vehicles such as cars, lorries and buses. However, vehicle engine and body parts made from aluminium resist rust and reduce the vehicle's weight. This enables lorries to carry heavier loads while staying under the legal weight limits that are in place to protect roads and bridges.

Go by train

Aluminium **alloys** are used extensively in railway carriages, underground trains and goods wagons. Less fuel is needed to move the trains because they are lighter. They also have better acceleration, which cuts down journey times. Carriages and wagons built from aluminium alloys last much longer than those built from steel because aluminium does not rust.

The '*1903 Flyer*'

The first aeroplane was designed and built by two brothers, Wilbur and Orville Wright. It flew 260 m near Kitty Hawk in North Carolina, on 14 December 1903. Although it was built around a wooden frame, its engine contained aluminium components to keep the weight down.

Into the air and beyond

Aluminium alloys are widely used in aircraft to make them as light as possible so they can get off the ground! The large external fuel tank on the Space Shuttle is made from a strong, but lightweight, alloy of aluminium containing four per cent copper and one per cent lithium. A similar alloy called duralumin is widely used in aircraft, cars and other machinery. Invented by Alfred Wilm early in the 20th century, duralumin consists of aluminium containing about four per cent copper, one per cent magnesium and a little manganese. It is easily worked into shape and becomes harder and stronger when heat-treated. As aluminium alloys resist corrosion, airlines sometimes do not paint their aircraft, which reduces the weight even further.

Airships

The largest airship ever built was the *Hindenburg*. Designed by Count von Zeppelin, it was 245 m long, had an aluminium frame and was kept in the air by 200,000 cubic metres of flammable hydrogen. In 1937 the *Hindenburg* exploded while coming into Lakehurst in New Jersey, USA. The hydrogen was blamed for the explosion, so modern airships use non-flammable helium. However, the frame was covered by fabric containing aluminium powder and iron oxide, the same mixture used to **weld** railway lines together, so the aluminium may have started the fire.

This is the famous airship, Hindenburg, which took four years to build and first flew in 1936. Its fabric skin contained aluminium powder and it had an aluminium alloy frame.

Aluminium compounds

Alumina or aluminium oxide is the white powder aluminium is **extracted** from. Another form of aluminium oxide is corundum, which forms attractive gemstones including rubies and sapphires. Rubies are red because they contain small amounts of chromium, whereas sapphires are blue because they have small amounts of titanium and iron. Artificial rubies and sapphires have been made since the beginning of the last century not just because they make attractive jewellery, but because they are very hard. The moving parts in mechanical watches often contain rubies to stop them being worn away.

The red circles you can see here are ruby jewels in the bearings of an expensive mechanical watch. Rubies are made from aluminium oxide and provide smooth, hard-wearing surfaces that reduce the friction between the moving parts in the watch.

The first laser

An American scientist called Theodore Maiman built the first laser in 1960. It used a ruby rod, and not surprisingly, produced a beam of red laser light.

Aluminium oxide

The form of aluminium oxide called corundum is one of the hardest natural substances. It is widely used in sandblasting, which is a method for cleaning buildings or to prepare the surface of steelwork ready for painting. It is also used as the abrasive in cutting and grinding tools for use on materials such as concrete.

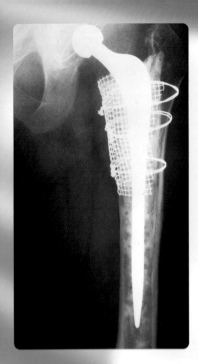

Aluminium oxide can be pressed into shape and heated to produce tough components that resist being worn away. The spark plugs in car engines contain aluminium oxide and artificial hip joints may be lined with it.

◀ *This x-ray photograph shows an artificial hip joint in place at the top of a leg. The hip is a ball-and-socket joint and the socket may be lined with aluminium oxide to provide a smooth, but tough, surface.*

Aluminium chloride

Aluminium chloride is a white solid used as a **catalyst** by industry for manufacturing chemicals like polystyrene. This is a plastic used to make cases for television sets and other electrical devices. Expanded polystyrene, containing bubbles of air, is used to make insulating containers for take-away foods. Hydrated aluminium chloride (also called aluminium chlorohydrate) is used in antiperspirants. Once it has been applied to the skin, it forms aluminium oxide, which plugs the pores in the skin, stopping the sweat getting out. Dry aluminium chloride is not used because it reacts with water to produce lots of heat and hydrochloric acid!

Aluminium hydroxide

Your stomach naturally contains hydrochloric acid to provide the acidic conditions you need to digest proteins. It also kills harmful bacteria that might be in your food. However, if your stomach produces too much acid you can get indigestion. Medicines called antacids help to cure indigestion by reacting with the extra acid. Aluminium hydroxide is often used as an antacid. When you swallow some, it reacts with the hydrochloric acid, helping you feel better.

The word equation for the reaction of aluminium hydroxide with hydrochloric acid is:

aluminium hydroxide + hydrochloric acid → aluminium chloride + water

Aluminium and living things

Water from rivers and reservoirs contains algae and tiny bits of various **minerals**. Before the water can be drunk these must be removed because they make the water cloudy and give it an unpleasant taste. Aluminium sulphate is used in water treatment plants as a flocculating agent, which means it sticks these bits together. The clumps of unwanted material are removed when the water is filtered, taking the aluminium sulphate with them. This is important because **soluble** aluminium **compounds** are poisonous to plants and animals.

The Camelford incident

In 1988 twenty tonnes of aluminium sulphate was accidentally tipped into the wrong tank at a water treatment plant, contaminating the water supply of the small English town of Camelford. The water tasted awful and was acidic because of the aluminium sulphate. The acid dissolved compounds of copper and other metals from the water pipes before they could be flushed clean, causing some people's hair and laundry to turn green or blue. Hundreds of people suffered skin rashes, arthritic pains and memory loss.

Aluminium and acid rain

Coal and oil contain sulphur compounds that produce sulphur dioxide gas when they are burned. If this gas escapes into the atmosphere, it dissolves in the clouds to produce acid rain. Rain is naturally acidic because it contains some dissolved carbon dioxide, but the sulphur dioxide can make it as acidic as lemon juice! The acid damages the waxy layer on leaves of trees and other plants and it dissolves aluminium compounds in the soil when it falls on the ground. Once the aluminium is dissolved, it is absorbed by plants through their roots, poisoning them. If aluminium gets washed into rivers and lakes, it can poison the animals and plants that live in them. If we are exposed to extra aluminium, our kidneys usually remove it from our bodies.

This girl (opposite) is receiving kidney dialysis treatment ▶
because her kidneys have failed. Modern dialysis is very safe, but
in the past dissolved aluminium compounds were sometimes
present in the dialysis fluid, which caused some patients to
suffer from temporary memory loss.

Acid rain has damaged these trees in a forest in North Carolina in the USA. The acid rain dissolves aluminium compounds from the soil, which poisons the trees and other plants.

Aluminium and dementia

Aluminium can build up in the bodies of people who suffer from kidney failure because their kidneys cannot filter waste substances from the blood properly. In the early days of dialysis, a process used to remove unwanted substances from blood, some people suffered from memory loss called 'dialysis dementia'. This was because the water used in the machines sometimes contained dissolved aluminium. Fortunately, dialysis dementia is reversible and modern dialyzing fluids do not contain aluminium.

Some people develop severe memory loss as they get older, called Alzheimer's disease. It is a very upsetting disease because eventually sufferers are unable to recognize their family or look after themselves. It was thought that aluminium caused Alzheimer's disease because it caused dialysis dementia. However, the two illnesses are very different and most scientists now believe that aluminium is not to blame.

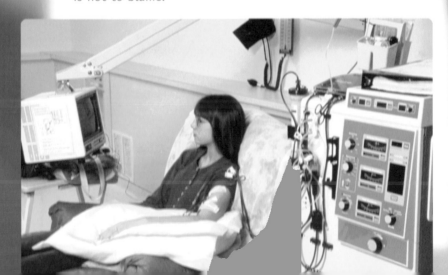

Gallium

Gallium is a silvery metal, soft enough to be cut with a knife. Gallium **reacts** slowly with acids, forming a layer of gallium oxide on its surface when it is exposed to air. This layer stops the gallium underneath from reacting with air and water.

Melts in the hand

Gallium has a very low melting point compared to most metals. It melts at just 29.7 °C, so you could melt some with the warmth from your hand. Most liquids contract when they are cooled and solidify. However, gallium expands, just as water does when it turns into ice.

▲
Gallium has a very low melting point compared with most metals. As you can see here, the warmth from a hand is enough to melt it.

Discovery of gallium

In 1875 Paul-Emile Lecoq studied the **spectrum** of light emitted by some zinc **ore** when it was heated and found two previously unknown violet lines. This suggested that an unknown **element** was present. Lecoq isolated gallium metal later that year by passing electricity through a solution of gallium hydroxide ($Ga(OH)_3$).

Eka-aluminium

*When Dimitri Mendeleev worked out his **periodic table** in 1871, he left gaps for elements that he thought had not yet been discovered. He left one gap below aluminium for a missing element that he called eka-aluminium, which means below aluminium. Mendeleev made predictions about the properties of eka-aluminium by looking at those of the surrounding elements in the periodic table. One of his predictions was that eka-aluminium would have a **density** of 5.9 g/cm^3. When gallium was discovered four years later, it was the missing eka-aluminium. Lecoq measured its density and found that it matched Mendeleev's predicted density almost exactly. This was a great success for Mendeleev's periodic table.*

Gallium in the ground

On average each tonne of rock in the Earth's crust contains just 19 g of gallium within various **compounds**. Gallium is found in rare **minerals** such as gallite (copper gallium sulphide) and sohngeite (gallium hydroxide). However, most gallium is **extracted** from bauxite, which is aluminium ore. On average, each tonne of bauxite contains about 50 g of gallium and this is taken out when the bauxite is purified ready for aluminium extraction. Only about a hundred tonnes of gallium are produced in the world each year. This might not sound like a lot, but it is mainly used for making electronic devices and only tiny amounts of gallium are needed.

This is a piece of bauxite. Most gallium is extracted from bauxite, which is actually an aluminium ore.

Uses of gallium

Mercury was used in most thermometers because it is liquid at room temperature and expands evenly when warmed up. Unfortunately, it is a poisonous metal, so other liquids such as alcohol are often used instead. Gallium's low melting point can be lowered even further if it is mixed with other metals. One such **alloy**, containing gallium, indium and tin, melts at −20 °C. It is used in a range of mercury-free thermometers for medical use, which are much safer than ordinary mercury thermometers. However, most gallium is used in making electronic devices.

Gallium arsenide

Gallium that contains tiny amounts of arsenic forms a **semiconductor** called gallium arsenide. This is a very important material because computer chips based on it are much quicker than those made using silicon. The biggest single use for gallium is to make fast electronic devices like radar transmitters. In addition, we can use gallium arsenide to make solar cells, light-emitting diodes (LEDs) and other electronic components because it is light-sensitive. This means that when light falls on gallium arsenide, it is converted into electricity, and conversely if electricity is passed through gallium arsenide, light is given off.

Gallium arsenide ▶
in used in fast computer chips for electronic devices such as radar.

Semiconductors and doping

Semiconductors are poor conductors of electricity at room temperature, but become better conductors at higher temperatures or when tiny amounts of other **elements** are added to them. This is called doping. Silicon, doped with elements such as gallium or arsenic, is the best known semiconductor. It is widely used to make 'silicon chips' for computers and other electronic devices.

Lovely light

Solar cells are devices that convert light (usually sunlight) directly into electricity and many of them contain gallium arsenide. Small solar cells are often used to power pocket calculators and many devices in remote areas, such as public telephone kiosks and road signs. Solar cells can only provide electricity while the Sun is shining on them, so rechargeable batteries are needed to keep the electricity flowing at night. In space, large panels made from many solar cells power satellites and space probes.

Small electronic components called light-emitting diodes (LEDs), contain materials such as gallium arsenide and gallium nitride. LEDs give off light when electricity is passed through them and are far more efficient than ordinary light bulbs because they release far less energy as heat. They are used in giant outdoor display screens, bicycle lights, and digital displays for electrical equipment such as video recorders. Lasers based on gallium arsenide are used in CD and DVD players to read the digital information on the disks.

▲
Gallium arsenide is used in many solar cells. In remote areas solar cells provide the electricity to power road signs and telephone kiosks, like this one in Nevada, USA.

Indium

Indium is a silvery metal that is softer than lead. It is easily worked into shape, even at very low temperatures. Indium does not **react** with oxygen in the air unless it is heated strongly and then it burns to form yellow indium oxide (In_2O_3). Although it reacts with acids, indium does not react with water.

▲
These are pieces of soft, silvery indium metal.

Discovery of indium

Indium was discovered in 1863 by Ferdinand Reich and Theodor Richter. During some chemical experiments on a sample of zinc **ore**, they made an unusual yellow solid, which led them to believe that the ore contained a new **element**. To confirm their discovery, Richter used a **spectroscope** to study the **spectrum** of light given off when the yellow solid was heated. The spectrum contained an indigo line.

Rare indium

There is very little indium in the Earth's crust. On average there may be less than a gram of indium in every ten tonnes of rock, so it is about as rare as silver. Indium is contained in rare **minerals** such as indite (iron indium sulphide), roquesite (copper indium sulphide) and dzhalindite (indium hydroxide). Over a third of the world's reserves of minerals that contain indium are found in Canada. Although China has smaller reserves of indium, it is the biggest producer of indium in the world. About three hundred tonnes of indium are produced in the world each year and a third of it comes from China. Indium is usually **extracted** from the waste material left over from processing zinc ore, especially sphalerite (zinc sulphide). The process is complex and involves several stages that take up to two months to complete! These include **electrolysis** and extraction with various chemicals. The indium extracted is mostly 99.97 per cent pure, but for electronic uses it may be further purified to 99.999 per cent or better.

Mirror, mirror ...

When indium melts, the molten metal clings easily to other substances, such as glass and metals. Mirrors are made by coating glass with molten aluminium or silver. When the metal solidifies it forms a shiny surface that reflects most of the light that falls on it, hardly changing the colour or shape at all. Mirrors made by coating glass with indium do not corrode easily, as silver does, and are even better at reflecting light than either aluminium or silver.

This is sphalerite (zinc sulphide), which is the main practical source of indium.

Uses of indium

Indium has some very unusual and useful properties. It is a metal that stays soft even at extremely low temperatures and it can stick to itself without needing to be heated first, a process called cold **welding**. A third of the indium produced is mixed with other metals to produce a wide range of **alloys** that also have many uses.

Brush regularly

If you have too many sweets and fizzy drinks, you may suffer from tooth decay. Although regular brushing helps, bacteria and the acids they produce may damage the hard outer layer of the tooth. Dentists remove the decayed part of the tooth and fill the hole left behind. Many modern tooth fillings are made from a white plastic material called resin. However, fillings made from a mixture of mercury, silver and other metals are still very common, as they are long-lasting and cheap. It is very important that the metal filling does not shrink as it hardens because any gaps left would let bacteria and acids back in, causing decay all over again. Small amounts of indium are used in the mixture to produce a hard alloy that shrinks very little.

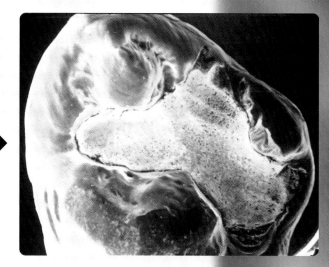

This is a tooth with a filling made from a mixture of mercury and silver, seen through an electron microscope. Metal dental fillings may also contain small amounts of indium to improve the properties of the filling.

Sticking and sealing

Many indium alloys melt at low temperatures, making them useful as solders for joining electronic components together. Electronic components are attached to printed circuit boards with an alloy, which contains 52 per cent indium and 48 per cent tin and melts at just 118 °C. This does not damage the components or the board because it melts at a low temperature.

Indium also resists corrosion. Indium alloys are also used in electrical fuses. If an electric device becomes faulty too much current could flow, which is dangerous. The high current causes the metal in the fuse to heat up and melt. This breaks the circuit and stops the electricity flowing.

Indium alloys are used as solders for joining electronic components together on printed circuit boards. They melt at low temperatures and do not corrode easily.

A strange alloy

Indium melts at 156 °C and gallium melts at 29.7 °C. However, a mixture of 24.5 per cent indium and 75.5 per cent gallium melts at just 16.5 °C! Indium alloys like this are useful for holding glass or plastic lenses while they are being ground to the correct shape because they can be released easily by gently warming the alloy.

It is often very difficult to get a tight seal between two different materials, such as metal and glass. When they are heated and cooled they expand and contract by different amounts, causing gaps to appear between them. However, indium sticks to metal and glass and forms a tight seal whether it is heated, cooled, or shaken about by vibrations. Indium seals are widely used in **vacuum** pumps and equipment that must work at low temperatures.

Indium compounds

Indium phosphide is a **semiconductor** material consisting of indium and tiny amounts of phosphorus. Like gallium arsenide, it is used in high-speed electronic circuits and solar cells. Only small amounts of indium are used in this way.

Indium-tin oxide

Special coatings that contain indium oxide account for about half of the indium produced. Very thin layers of indium oxide are transparent and can conduct electricity. Indium-tin oxide (ITO) contains about 90 per cent indium oxide and ten per cent tin oxide. ITO conducts electricity better than indium oxide on its own and thin layers of it are also transparent. These properties make ITO a very useful material in many ways.

No more frosty windows

In winter, windows of vehicles can become coated on the outside with thick frost. When we get inside, things often get even worse, water vapour in our breath condenses on the glass, 'misting up' the windows and making it impossible to see out. ITO-coated glass is easily de-iced and de-misted within a short time, just by passing electricity from the car battery through the ITO layer. The ITO layer does not interfere with visibility, as it is transparent. This glass is widely used in train and aircraft windscreens and for making 'frost-free' glass doors for commercial food freezers.

The windscreens of trains, aeroplanes and helicopters may be coated with a very thin, transparent layer of indium-tin oxide. When electricity is passed through the layer, it warms up and removes any frost or 'mist' from the glass, providing a clear view in cold weather.

Keep your cool

Buildings with lots of windows can become unbearably hot in the summer because infrared light from the Sun passes through the glass into the rooms. We cannot see infrared light, but we do feel it as heat. Thin layers of indium-tin oxide let visible light through, but stop infrared light. Buildings that have ITO-coated glass in the windows warm up less in the summer because the infrared light that passes through the windows is reduced. It is more comfortable inside and there is less need to use air-conditioning equipment. As a result, energy is not wasted trying to keep the building cool.

Liquid crystal displays

Liquid crystal displays (LCDs) are used in all sorts of electrical devices. These include the flat screens used in laptop computers, CD players, electronic hand-held games, digital watches and calculators. When light passes through liquid crystals it is twisted. However when electricity flows through liquid crystals, they change shape and cannot twist the light as much, producing a dark area in the display. One of the layers in the display is ITO-coated glass, which conducts electricity to the liquid crystals. Some computer displays are touch-sensitive and can detect your finger when you touch the screen. These have a thin coating of ITO on the outer surface.

◀ *Liquid crystal displays (LCDs) contain a layer of glass coated with indium-tin oxide. LCDs are widely used in calculators, digital watches, CD players and other electronic devices.*

Thallium

Thallium is a soft metal. It **reacts** with oxygen in the air to form a thick layer of blue-grey thallium oxide. However, if this is cut away the surface is silvery with a blue tinge. Thallium does not react with water, but it does with steam to form thallium hydroxide and hydrogen gas. Thallium reacts slowly with acids such as sulphuric and hydrochloric acids.

Not three, just one

When **elements** in **group** 3 react with other elements such as chlorine, the **compounds** formed have a similar chemical formula. Boron chloride is BCl_3 and aluminium chloride is $AlCl_3$, for example. However, thallium compounds are different. Thallium chloride, for instance, is $TlCl$, just one chlorine **atom** for each thallium atom instead of three.

Discovery of thallium

The English scientist Sir William Crookes discovered thallium in 1861. Crookes was actually interested in selenium compounds and was heating some waste left over from sulphuric acid production, which is where selenium is normally found. When he examined the **spectrum** of light produced he found an unexpected green line. It wasn't selenium that Crookes had found, but a new element, which he named thallium after the Greek word meaning green twig. Crookes and a French chemist called Claude-Auguste Lamy both managed to isolate thallium in 1862 and each showed that it was a metal.

This is the English scientist Sir William Crookes (1832–1919), who discovered thallium in 1861 and invented a radiometer. He is seen here holding another one of his inventions, the Crookes tube, which he used to investigate cathode rays. ▶

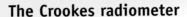

The Crookes radiometer

William Crookes measured the atomic mass of thallium using a **vacuum** balance. However when light shone on it he got slightly different readings. He investigated this further and as a result he invented his 'radiometer'. This is a glass bulb containing very little air and a rotor with four metal vanes. One side of each vane is black and the other side is shiny. When sunlight shines on the vanes, the black sides warm up more than the shiny sides. The air **molecules** next to the black sides absorb some of the heat and bounce off the vanes, causing the rotor to spin very quickly. The Crookes radiometer has little practical use, but is an interesting toy.

Thallium production

Thallium compounds are found in several rare **minerals** such as crooksite, lorandite and hutchinsonite, but the pure metal is not found naturally. Thallium is rare in the Earth's crust and on average each tonne of rock contains only about half a gram of thallium compounds. Only about fifteen tonnes of thallium and its compounds are **extracted** in the world each year. Rather than trying to extract thallium from its minerals, it is obtained from waste material left over after zinc production, just like indium. Several steps are needed and thallium metal is eventually produced by passing electricity through a solution of thallium compounds.

Uses of thallium

Thallium metal itself has no real commercial use. An **alloy** of mercury and thallium is used in thermometers for measuring low temperatures because it freezes at −59 °C, 20 °C lower than mercury on its own. Most thallium is used in various thallium **compounds**.

Bending light

When a ray of light passes from one transparent substance into another, for instance, from air into glass, it changes direction slightly. This is called refraction. The larger the 'refractive index' of the transparent substance the more the light bends. Lenses are shaped in such a way that the light is focused. They are important parts of many things including spectacles, microscopes and telescopes. Glass containing thallium oxide has a larger refractive index than ordinary glass, so it bends light more, allowing thinner lenses to be made.

The thalofide cell

Thallium sulphide (Tl_2S) forms blue-black crystals, which are used in some photocells. These are electronic devices that are sensitive to light. When light shines on the photocell, a small electric current flows, which stops when the light source is removed. The thalofide cell was invented in 1917 by two Americans, Theodore Case and Earl Sponable and is sensitive to infrared light. Thalofide cells contain thallium oxy-sulphide, which is thallium sulphide with some sulphur **atoms** replaced by oxygen atoms. They were used by the US Navy during World War I as part of a secret signalling system based on invisible, infrared light. Simple Morse code was used at first, but the system was later developed to carry voice signals between ships nearly 20 km (12.5 miles) apart.

Infrared spectroscopy

Infrared **spectroscopy** is a method used by chemists to analyze chemicals. Various chemicals absorb infrared light in different ways and every chemical has its own 'fingerprint'. Crystals containing thallium bromide and thallium iodide are very good at letting infrared light pass through. They are used to make lenses and other parts of infrared spectroscopes.

Not just movies – talkies too!

Case and Sponable's thalofide cell was the basis of 'Movietone', one of the first methods for adding sound to movies. The sound track was recorded as a series of dark lines on one side of the film. When the film was shown, a thalofide cell converted the pattern of lines into a series of electrical pulses, which were used to power a loudspeaker. The first 'Movietone News' stories, complete with sound, were shown in 1927.

Gamma-ray detectors

Gamma rays are similar to X-rays, but more powerful. They are found in cosmic rays from space, so astronomers are very interested in studying them. Sodium iodide crystals containing small amounts of thallium emit a flash of light whenever gamma rays go through them. They are used in gamma-ray detectors in space probes and gamma-ray telescopes.

▼ Gamma rays can be detected using sodium iodide crystals, containing small amounts of thallium. Such crystals were used in this space telescope, called the Compton Gamma Ray Observatory, which was launched into orbit from the Space Shuttle in 1991.

Thallium and health

Thallium is a **dense** metal and one of its **compounds**, thallium ethanoate, is used to make liquids with a high density. These liquids are used by the metal r**efining** industry to separate the different **minerals** in **ores**. Crushed rock is mixed with the dense liquid and lots of bubbles are blown through. This produces froth at the surface that contains some minerals, while others sink to the bottom. However, soluble thallium compounds like this must be handled carefully, as they are poisonous.

Ringworm and rats

Ringworm is in fact a fungal skin infection that causes itchy red rashes that look like rings. It is quite contagious and is spread by contact with infected pets, people, combs and clothing. Modern antifungal creams help to treat ringworm safely, but in the past thallium ethanoate and thallium sulphate were used. Although they were effective, they were also poisonous and were often used as rat poison too!

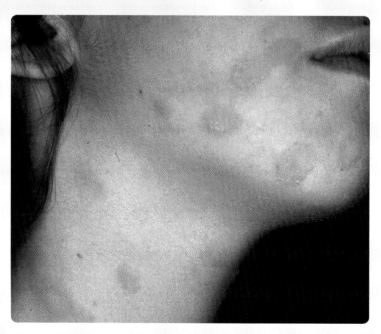

▲
The red rings on this person's skin are caused by a fungal infection called ringworm. Thallium compounds such as thallium sulphate were used to cure ringworm in the past, but they are no longer used because they are too poisonous.

Poisonous thallium

Many countries have banned the use of thallium compounds if safer alternatives exist. In 1972 the USA banned the use of thallium compounds in rat poison and they are not used to treat ringworm any more. If someone swallows a large dose of thallium compound, they suffer from vomiting, diarrhoea and possibly hair loss after about two weeks. In severe cases they may die. However, thallium is still used in modern medicine.

Thallium in cardiac scans

Thallium-201 is an artificial **isotope**, which is **radioactive** and gives off **radiation**, such as X-rays. It is used by doctors to study the blood flow of patients with heart disease. When a patient has a cardiac scan with thallium-201, a tiny amount is injected into a vein – the needle causes the only pain! The thallium-201 goes wherever the blood flows and the radiation it emits is easily detected by a hand-held scanner. The doctor may compare a scan of the heart after the patient has exercised on a treadmill with one taken while the patient is resting. This helps the doctor find out if there are any areas in the heart not getting enough blood.

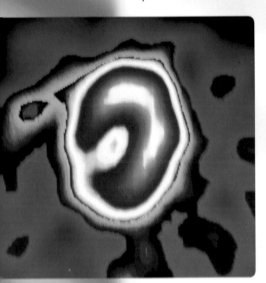

◀ *This is a thallium scan of a normal human heart. The pink and red areas show where the thallium has concentrated in the heart muscle. Scans like this help doctors diagnose problems that may lead to heart attacks.*

Isotopes

*Isotopes are **atoms** of an **element** that have the same number of **protons** and **electrons**, but different numbers of **neutrons**. Most elements found naturally have a small number of different isotopes mixed together, but scientists are able to make artificial isotopes in nuclear reactors and machines called particle accelerators.*

Find out more about the group 3 elements

The table below contains information about the properties of the **group 3 elements**.

Element	Symbol	Atomic number	Melting point (°C)	Boiling point (°C)	State at 25 °C	State at 30 °C	Density at 25°C (g/cm³)
boron	B	5	2076	3927	solid	solid	2.3
aluminium	Al	13	660	2520	solid	solid	2.7
gallium	Ga	31	29.7	2403	solid	liquid	5.9
indium	In	49	156	2072	solid	solid	7.3
thallium	Tl	81	304	1473	solid	solid	11.8

Compounds

These tables show you the chemical formulae of most of the **compounds** mentioned in this book. For example, boron oxide has the formula B_2O_3. This means it is made from two boron **atoms** and three oxygen atoms, joined together by chemical **bonds**.

Boron compounds

Boron compounds	formula
borax	$Na_2B_4O_7.10H_2O$
colemanite	$CaB_3O_4(OH)_3.H_2O$
kernite	$Na_2B_4O_6(OH)_2.3H_2O$
boric acid	H_3BO_3
boron carbide	B_4C
boron chloride	BCl_3
boron nitride	BN
boron oxide	B_2O_3
diborane	B_2H_6
sodium borate	Na_3BO_3

Aluminium compounds	formula
bauxite	Al_2O_3
cryolite	Na_3AlF_6
aluminium chloride	$AlCl_3$
aluminium chlorohydrate	$AlCl_3.6H_2O$
aluminium hydroxide	$Al(OH)_3$
aluminium oxide	Al_2O_3
aluminium sulphate	$Al_2(SO_4)_3$
potassium aluminium sulphate	$KAl(SO_4)_2.12H_2O$

Gallium compounds	formula
gallite	$CuGaS_2$
sohngeite	$Ga(OH)_3$
gallium arsenide	$GaAs$
gallium nitride	GaN

Indium compounds	formula
dzhalindite	$In(OH)_3$
indite	$Fe^{2+}In_2S_4$
roquesite	$CuInS_2$
indium oxide	In_2O_3
indium phosphide	InP

Thallium compounds	formula
thallium chloride	$TlCl$
crooksite	$Cu_7(Tl,Ag)Se_4$
lorandite	$TlAsS_2$
hutchinsonite	$(Pb,Tl)_2As_5S_9$
thallium ethanoate	CH_3COOTl
thallium iodide	TlI
thallium bromide	$TlBr$
thallium hydroxide	$TlOH$
thallium oxide	Tl_2O
thallium sulphide	Tl_2S
thallium sulphate	Tl_2SO_4

Find out more continued

Acids

Acids	formula
boric acid	H_3BO_3
hydrochloric acid	HCl
nitric acid	HNO_3
sulphuric acid	H_2SO_4

Other compounds

Other compounds	formula
ammonia	NH_3
ammonium perchlorate	NH_4ClO_4
iron oxide	Fe_2O_3
sodium iodide	NaI
tin oxide	SnO
water	H_2O
zinc sulphide	ZnS

◀ This is sphalerite (zinc sulphide), which is the main practical source of indium.

Glossary

alloy mixture of two or more metals or mixture of a metal and a non-metal. Alloys are often more useful than the pure metal on its own.

atom smallest particle of an element that has the properties of that element. An atom contains smaller particles called subatomic particles.

atomic number number of protons in the nucleus of an atom. It is also called the proton number. No two elements have the same atomic number.

bond force that joins atoms together

compound substance made from the atoms of two or more elements, joined together by chemical bonds. Compounds can be broken down into simpler substances and they have different properties from the elements in them. Water, for example, is a liquid at room temperature, but it is made from two gases, hydrogen and oxygen.

density mass of a substance compared to its volume. To work out the density of a substance, you divide its mass by its volume. Substances with a high density feel very heavy for their size.

DNA (deoxyribonucleic acid) complex, long-chained chemical, which carries genetic information and is the substance of inheritance for almost all living things. It is found in the cell nucleus.

electrolysis breaking down or decomposing a compound by passing electricity through it. The compound must be molten or dissolved in a liquid for electrolysis to work.

electron subatomic particle with a negative electric charge. Electrons are found around the nucleus of an atom.

element substance made from one type of atom. Elements cannot be broken down into simpler substances. All substances are made from one or more elements.

extract remove a chemical from a mixture of chemicals

fertilizer chemical that gives plants the elements they need for healthy growth

group vertical column of elements in the periodic table. Elements in a group have similar properties.

herbicide chemical that kills unwanted plants, usually weeds

isotope atom of an element with the same number of protons and electrons as other atoms of the same element, but different numbers of neutrons. Different isotopes share the same atomic number.

mineral substance that is found naturally, but does not come from animals or plants. Metal ores and limestone are examples of minerals.

neutron subatomic particle with no electric charge. Neutrons are found in the nucleus of an atom.

nuclear reaction reaction involving the nucleus of an atom. Radiation is produced in nuclear reactions.

nucleus part of an atom made from protons and neutrons. It has a positive electric charge and is found at the centre of the atom.

ore mineral from which metals can be taken out and purified

period horizontal row of elements in the periodic table

periodic table table in which all the known elements are arranged into groups and periods

pesticide chemical that kills insects

prism block of transparent material, usually glass, which has a triangular cross-section

proton subatomic particle with a positive electric charge. Protons are found in the nucleus of an atom.

proton number number of protons in the nucleus of an atom. It is also called the atomic number. No two elements have the same proton number.

radiation energy or particles given off when an atom decays

radioactive describes a substance that can produce radiation

reaction chemical change that produces new substances

refining removing impurities from a substance to make it more pure. It can also mean separating the different substances in a mixture, for example, in oil refining.

semiconductor substance that is an electrical insulator at room temperature, but a conductor when it is warmed or other elements are added to it

soluble substance that will dissolve in water

spectroscope piece of equipment that splits the light given off by something into its spectrum

spectrum different colours that make up a ray of light. Different colours of light have different spectra.

subatomic particle particle smaller than an atom, such as a proton, neutron or an electron

vacuum empty space containing very little air or none at all

welding joining two or more metals together, usually by heating them

Timeline

boron discovered	1808	Sir Humphry Davy, Joseph-Louis Gay-Lussac and Louis-Jaques Thénard
aluminium discovered	1825	Hans Christian Oersted
thallium discovered	1861	Sir William Crookes
indium discovered	1863	Ferdinand Reich and Theodor Richter
gallium discovered	1875	Paul-Emile Lecoq
industrial extraction of aluminium invented	1886	Charles Hall and Paul Héroult
first laser built	1960	Theodore Maiman

Further reading and useful websites

Books

Knapp, Brian, *The Elements* series, particularly, *Aluminium* (Atlantic Europe Publishing Co., 1996)

Oxlade, Chris, *Chemicals in Action* series, particularly, *Elements and Compounds* (Heinemann Library, 2002)

Oxlade, Chris, *Chemicals in Action: Metals* (Heinemann Library, 2002)

Websites

WebElements™
http://www.webelements.com
An interactive periodic table crammed with information and photographs.

DiscoverySchool
http://school.discovery.com/clipart
Help for science projects and homework and free science clip art.

Proton Don
http://www.funbrain.com/periodic
The fun periodic table quiz!

BBC Science
http://www.bbc.co.uk/science
Quizzes, news, information and games about all areas of science.

Creative Chemistry
http://www.creative-chemistry.org.uk
An interactive chemistry site with fun practical activities, quizzes, puzzles and more.

Index

Titles in the *Periodic Table* series include:

Hardback   0 431 16995 0

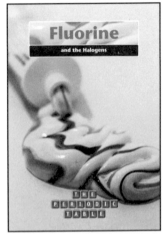

Hardback   0 431 16997 7

Hardback   0 431 16998 5

Hardback   0 431 16996 9

Hardback   0 431 16994 2

Hardback   0 431 16999 3

Find out about the other titles in this series on our website www.heinemann.co.uk/library